Book 6

Sentience changed *everything...*

We just weren't paying attention

Whickwithy

Book 6

Published by Whickwithy
whickwithy@gmail.com

ISBN: 978-1-7348221-2-0

Book 6 by Whickwithy

First published Spring 2022
Mid November, 2022 Edition

Previous efforts:
Sentience
A Sentient Perspective
Beauty & Fiction
Millennium

An animal's life is what it was given.   Human life is what we make of it. Prehuman life is all that we have attained.

"Education of the mind without education of the heart is no education at all" (it is *prehuman*)
  -Aristotle

"When will our consciences grow so tender that we will act to prevent human misery rather than avenge it?"
  - Eleanor Roosevelt

Answer: when we become human.

The Road Foreword

Darwin's theory does not take conscious awareness into account. It is the next step in evolution. We change ourselves at a level far beyond the scope of genetics by consciously being aware of what is going on around us and changing to adapt.

We missed the most important necessary change because we forced our conscious awareness into our subconscious.

If, as you look around, you are convinced this is the best that humanity can do, I am horrified.

Monsters in charge. Equality of any kind nonexistent but, *especially* between the genders. The mind-boggling belief that *forcing* equality can actually ever create equality.

The mealy-mouthed version of love that everyone accepts.

Humanity is far more than that.

SMH

Human Nature

Whether we like it or not, sentience changed everything. We have never understood the full impact of sentient awareness on humanity. Conscious awareness, the most important facet of our sentient state has been hampered during our long journey from animal to human.

The phrase "perception is reality" is a warning, not an observation. Our faulty perceptions are due to the millions of years of inertia of the animal's perspective which we have followed blindly.

Sentience is about *clarifying* reality, not interpreting it to suit the animal's limited understanding. We have garbled *human* reality with relics that remain from the animal. We find human *nature* in conflict with the human *condition* because of this.

For more than four thousand years, we have all been attending disorientation training from the day we are born. The animal has been the trainer-in-charge.

As we systematically attempt to destroy our world seems a good time to explore and align the human condition with human nature. Realign *away* from our animal legacy.

The conflict was set as soon as we learned to ask the question, "why?" and began to seek answers. That was our conscious awareness coming to the fore.

All of the worthier characteristics of humanity, such as honor, integrity, etc are inherent in human nature. They are run into the ground by our current prehuman situation.

Our current condition destroys the self-respect necessary to maintain the natural, noble characteristics of the evolved human.

Human *nature* is loving. The *prehuman* condition is not. We find ourselves caught in the disorienting maze of an animal's perceptions. Distortions to the human condition were assured as soon as we obfuscated and obscured the simple answer to one crucial question. What is love?

Sentience is due to our conscious awareness, even more than our intelligence. We have forcefully ignored what our heightened awareness has been telling us.

Our minds have been educated but our hearts have not.

Shouting "love is good" is not enough. While true, shouting it does not achieve a loving state. The same goes for the phrase, "I love you". Words and good intentions, alone, do not fulfill either concept. It is like a child pouting.

The phrases exist due to the intuitive sense of our suppressed conscious awareness. Awareness of human reality has been forced into our subconscious. We bandy the word love about without understanding. Three thousand years prove that beyond a doubt.

The deceptions we have created are legend. The animal legacy endures. In the absence of that which unleashes our human nature we remain a demented animal.

We accept all of the misery, frustration, inanity, and insanity of the prehuman condition as if it were meant to be. We never even question why we remain such a miserable race. We accept what is not acceptable.

The *pre*human *condition* is ruled by our animal legacy. Unleashed conscious awareness will lead us through the maze of animal madness to discover our human *nature*.

The laws we put in place only contain the worst offenses of the confounded animal and not very well at that. They allow us to poorly *mimic* human nature. Very poorly at that.

Laws attempt to *force* good behavior on the *animal*. It is only the training of Pavlov's dog. They don't change the animal into a human. Our humanity needs to be unleashed.

Our *human nature* needs to take the lead. Humanity needs to become human, not just act out the part. It turns out we are lousy actors. We follow a vague, unfinished script.

The big picture *must* be considered. We chase individual, superficial problems with laws and such rather than explore what is completely missing from the human equation.

What makes the human condition equal to our loving human nature? What creates love?

We have been treating humanity like an animal to be trained, "Bad dog!" We need to accept what has been missing all along.

Laws were essentially an overly intelligent animal's way in which to address a human problem. Our conscious awareness had not yet caught up. It had been, and still is, sidelined.

The noble characteristics of humanity need to be liberated, not mimicked. The problems we attack through laws do not address the fundamental issues that wreak havoc on our human nature. The *pre*human condition constantly morphs to adapt (e.g. don't get caught, find a loophole), not overcome.

We remain in a no-man's land beyond the animal's ken and well short of human nature's capacity.

If you look at the human condition, it makes no sense. We have everything ... except reason and emotional stability, the mainstays of a sane human existence.

We have suppressed what our conscious awareness makes abundantly apparent. Our perceptions must match reality . Our reason and emotional stability remain forfeit.

Nature's intent has always been to develop a race that could sense and adjust to its surroundings and circumstances in such a way that it can transform itself.

Our highly developed sentient awareness has been blunted into submission to a blind mania for more than three millennia.

Transformation

There is one situation that causes our emotions, reason, and understanding to go completely haywire. Because of that, we have never faced a distressing situation that has always been apparent. We ran for cover, instead.

Sex has been around for a *billion* years. It is well known. Love has been around a few *thousand*. It is not understood at all. Love is a term that remains garbled, muddled, and confused.

Coitus is a certainty for humanity. It is the only form of sexual activity that makes babies. It puts life into life. Literally.

The *sentient* intent of coitus baffled our conscious awareness as we evolved from an animal. This is not surprising since sex had been around for a billion years and love was a new concept.

Coitus, in its human form, is about loving. In its finished form, coitus is an incredible, transcendent experience *for both*.

Is coitus for love/mutual pleasure or making babies? The only answer that suits our sentient nature is *both*. Our sentience makes us well aware of the fact that coitus should be a fully shared pleasure. Orgasms should be mutual. That is why we call it making love, even though it is seldom the case today.

For the animal, just making babies is fine. Love and mutual orgasm was never a consideration.

Those most intent have found many ways around the limitation. But, never straight through.

Long, long ago, attaining loving coitus seemed hopeless. In embarrassment, it was forced into the subconscious, never to be considered seriously, again, *for no good reason*. The quest was abandoned too soon.

Our early ancestors had not the wit to make coitus into a loving act, so they buried it rather than face the stark failure. Babies were *still* required. Coitus *had to* continue. It became a self-reinforcing disaster. The situation was desperately buried further beneath distractions, deceits, and delusions over the following millennia. We were unwilling to face the truth without an answer. *Because* we were never willing to face the truth of the situation, we never found the answer.

If you spend any time thinking about it, if your mind doesn't veer away from the consideration, as is the usual case, it is obvious that the goal is easily attained.

We are an intelligent, fully capable sentient race. More importantly, Nature, of course, provided for the eventuality of the sentient requirement. It is shocking that it took us three millennia to realize this.

Until coitus becomes a consistently loving event, we will remain a miserable, befuddled and demented animal, well short of our human potential.

Our sentience tells us it is possible. Our animal history assures us it is not. That shattered our minds. As a newly hatched sentient race, we could not reconcile what a billion years had told us about coitus with what our sentience *knew* to be true. The most important transition from the animal fell to our limited experience as a sentient race.

Nature created us in in every to assure it was possible to love as a sentient being expects. From our intellect to our conscious awareness, and physical form, nature provided.

It is the crucial breakaway step from the animal. *Mutual* orgasm is the foundation of love. It makes us human.

The question we have never asked openly derails our sanity and sentience still today. "How does unassisted coitus become the glorious, celebrated, and fulfilling act that it should be?" We engaged in skullduggery, instead.

We would have discovered and resolved this issue long ago if we had not been so afraid of confronting it ... and failing. It was a survival mechanism to assure the ongoing fulfillment of the need for babies in the absence of resolution. There was no regard for what it did to our conscious awareness, our humanity.

Understandable at the time but, still, devastating to our progress as a sentient race. It lasted too long and became intertwined with deceit and delusion. The answer adopted long ago was "there's nothing to be done. Don't even think about it."

Thinking is what a sentient race does, whether we like it or not. Attempting to avoid the stark situation, damaged our ability to think. The awareness *clearly* cannot be avoided, but we forced it into our subconscious, never to be heard from again for millennia.

Coitus is an act of procreation but it also developed in such a way that humans can adapt it to fulfill their need for sharing at a level beyond the capability of any living being before humanity.

Bafflement and fear shut down our humanity and our sentient awareness in its tracks.

Love remains on life support. We carry on as an animal with far too much brains and not enough sense to match. We remain *very* unstable. Our emotional state remains a shambles.

Men take and women give. It starts in bed. That is the prehuman condition as it fails to overcome the animal's inertia and adapt to its sentient nature.

A baffling aspect regarding that which laid men low and creates so much toxic behaviour is the failure to *provide* orgasm.

That is a massive misdirect. It confused the whole issue. If men achieve orgasm, what in the world could they be unhappy about? Even men have had a hard time understanding.

Do you not see? Even though the man would love to do otherwise, the failure to achieve the woman's orgasm forces the act of coitus to become a selfish effort. It cripples his sentient sense of self, thus damaging the noble characteristic of his human nature. Self-respect is permanently undermined for the vast majority of men from the time they reach puberty. He remains an animal.

Self-respect is necessary for the noble characteristics of a sentient being to flourish.

The obverse has been just as confounding to the animal mentality and startling to our human, conscious awareness as it finally becomes clear.

Women give *everything* and get nothing in return more than 75% of the time. It would seem this should cause toxicity.

Think about it for a minute. It all makes sense. It is the way loving works. *The loving is in the giving.* The giving is the key.

Ironically, it is not the lack of orgasm that initially repulses women. It is the men's lack of human behavior that so disturbs.

Men take and women give. It all starts in bed. Nature always meant coitus to become a loving act to fulfill the sentient state. Men and women must *both* know how to give.

The most important point is that men must learn to give. It begins in bed. The architecture of love has no foundation until men overcome their fear of failure and realize there was never any reason to fear. Reciprocal loving can flourish and grow. It is dead easy once we overcome the spineless fear.

The biggest problem we have with coitus, and sex in general, is that we are too embarrassed to discuss it, think about it, or even acknowledge it. Our sentience is in constant rebellion against our inability to transform coitus into an act of love. The all-encompassing conundrum we have never faced openly is that all of us really, really want to give *and* receive sexual orgasm.

Now, at last, we can learn the basis of love in its most essential form and make it happen (more on that later). Shouting "love is good" is not enough. We must fulfill the most essential basis for sentient existence that Nature granted us.

As one looks further, the deception becomes even more stunning and destructive. Many men do not realize that the problem exists on a wide scale. Many think it is only them and a few others that endure the misery of failure. That is exactly what all of the fiction that we consume implies. It is not so. Most couples never achieve mutually orgasmic coitus.

The belief that it is rare has crippled us even further. It is the source of most of the paranoia and misanthropy we endure as a man grows to perceive that he is isolated and alone with his problem.

It is *not* a personal problem. 75% to *95%* of unassisted coitus is *not* mutually orgasmic, no matter what the movies and other forms of fiction tell you. That is not enough for a sentient race. It shatters everything about our sentient existence.

The situation has wrought havoc on the prehuman condition since the beginning. Our conscious awareness remains blinded to our awful state and the wonder of humanity that can be ours.

Even more mind-boggling is that many women blame themselves for the failure. Just to be clear, the man must learn to last longer and he can. It's dead easy. Only because we ran away from the situation has it lasted for so very, very long to our lasting dismay and discouragement.

Only a sentient being can sense the incongruity and dysfunction of prehuman coitus. More importantly, we *cannot avoid sensing it*. We have to deal with it or remain unstable.

Humanity can do better. So, why haven't we? Before we even begin to speak, we are taught to avoid any thought on the subject. That has gone on for thousands of years. We are in a stupour regarding the most essential act of love. It renders our conscious awareness meaningless.

Every generation wakes up to the fact but can't express it. Each generation rebels in its youth as they reach puberty with no idea regarding what they are rebelling against. We just sense that something is wrong. The preconditioning shunts all further thought on the subject aside.

As the situation persists without resolution, we fall in line with all of the previous generations of prehumans. We embrace the misery.

As we age further, at least at a subconscious level, we realize we have been had. That is when e*verything* begins to turn foul.

Most every man that ever lived has not been able to *share* the most incredible experience of his existence. He is trained into believing that *he cannot give*. It begins in bed.

Until coitus becomes a loving act, it remains a selfish act for the man. It implodes his self-respect. Selfishness inadvertently became deemed a dominant trait in the male gender.

It is not genetic, it's not coincidence and it is not "just the way men are". It is only the reaction to the failure to make coitus into shared loving. *None to blame. But, everyone to pity. Men need to learn to give.*

We have continued to avoid resolution due to three thousand years of confusion, embarrassment, stupour, and misery.

Humanity donned a shadowy cloak regarding the *sentient* intent that is mutual orgasm during unassisted coitus.

Pursuing mutual orgasm in any other form has been demonized and persecuted by the dull-witted tyranny of the animal mentality. Anyone daring to explore any other way in which to provide for the loving necessity has been victimized because of this misunderstanding.

In the absence of resolution, any other way in which to achieve the sharing of love has been feared and dreaded. The dull-witted state of our ancestors deemed that coitus could not compete. In confusion, alternatives were feared.

Coitus will continue. It's just that, for humanity to become human, coitus must become human, also.

The emergence of our conscious awareness revealed that coitus was incomplete and unfulfilling. We shunted the thought aside, along with our humanity, long before we could put the pieces of the puzzle together and realize it need not remain so.

Any consideration of the woman's interest in orgasm was a quandary for our newly evolved awareness. Procreation was required to continue. Anything that threatened that was an existential threat. Do you begin to see the snarly mess our ancient ancestors faced?

Our sentience remains aware of the situation, even when shunted to the subconscious. The subjugated conscious awareness haunts us throughout our lifetime.

Absence of reciprocal loving becomes a burden for a sentient race. Animals slog along doing the same old thing, no matter what. Humans have the remarkable ability to recognize and adjust their circumstances. We have not even attempted to apply that ability where it is *most crucial*.

Unlearning that which make coitus a sentient failure is simple. The much more difficult task is unlearning all of the nonsense that we have all been fed since birth. The nonsense has increased and been embellished for three millennia. It keeps us from ever broaching the question.

"Just don't talk about it" is a mantra that was conceived thousands of years ago. "Just don't think about it" is invoked every time coitus fails to be a mutually orgasmic act of love. It is easier to go to sleep and forget about it by morning.

We continue to act like everything is okay.

The self-deception is the foundation for so much that we despise about our prehuman condition. The failure of loving coitus has stalled the fulfillment of our human nature. More so, it has stunted and distorted our human nature. The failure of human, sentient, loving coitus has *caused* the whacky, distorted views that we see on full display in the 2020's. If you think about it at all, you will know it is true.

Men don't ever lose their drive for the ultimate sexual pleasure which is so easily theirs and, yet, so difficult for them to share. Do you begin to see how that, along with the need for babies, muddled the picture beyond recognition for our witless ancestors?

Do you think a human, sentient mind can *avoid* awareness of the failure that is repeated endlessly throughout a lifetime? Do you think any human, sentient mind *wants* to fail at love??!!!?

It has been gnawing on men's minds for at least three thousand years as well as wearing away women's patience and gnawing away at the sentience that is naturally theirs.

Why do men wreak so much havoc? It's not testosterone as is the usual excuse. That just exacerbates the situation. It is the devastating disappointment caused by the failure to achieve the sentient grace of providing the most incredible experience to another. The sentient grace that is easily and naturally fulfilled by the woman.

Women's naturally growing lack of interest over a lifetime in something that is only minimally pleasurable is another element that exacerbates the situation. Do you see where the conflict grows over the life of a relationship?

A tension is created underlying every aspect of the prehuman condition. It starts in the home and the heart. From there, it infiltrates every other aspect of our existence.

It is so devastating that it compromises most men's humanity within a few years and grind away at what's left for the rest of his life. The woman often ends up looking for somewhere to hide.

It also leads to the constantly growing schism between men and women on the larger scale.

It ameliorates the devastation, to a great extent, if a man finds some way in which to satisfy a woman. The same is true of any way in which two humans achieve mutual orgasm. Any way to achieve mutual orgasm is more human than not. It is the basis of love. Without it, *at best*, love withers over the years.

But, there is only one coitus. So, why should it remain lacking? Coitus cannot be eliminated if the human race desires to remain extant.

If it were not possible to make coitus into a loving act, then assuring that every sexual engagement was mutually orgasmic in some way would be in order. That is much more difficult to achieve than making the most natural act of life into a loving art.

The lack of loving coitus affects each gender but in different ways. The only thing shared is mass confusion and frustration. It is devastating to the human condition.

Sadly, as we remain in our prehuman condition, women are adopting more of the offensive and violent characteristics of the demented male. We are learning to live like an animal in the absence of the common availability of the very human desire for loving coitus. We never become truly human and sentient without it.

There is no reason that the the act of coitus should remain anything less than a spectacular success for a sentient race. It's too important.

Now, I can state confidently and unequivocally that, "It's all about the glands." Men can easily learn to make loving coitus. I explain the details later in this book.

So, on with our humanity.

The Big Picture

Gazing into the eyes of your lover as you each reach ecstasy, sharing that incredible feeling with another. It's special. It releases our human nature as opposed to our animal legacy.

Loving coitus rearranges the prehuman condition into something much more closely resembling our human nature. We have struggled so long to accept and fulfill our human nature because the most crucial element, that which can clearly distinguish man from animal, the attainment of the physical expression of love, has been missing in its most natural form.

It's incredible. It is only the lack of realizing that it was possible that derailed our attainment of the the most crucial aspect of the human experience.

We hid the devastating conclusion of failure from our conscious awareness and excused it in nonsensical fashion like a befuddled animal, which our most ancient ancestors most certainly were. That crippled our conscious awareness regarding all of existence.

We have pulled every trick in the book to avoid consciously realizing we are lousy at coitus. We forced ourselves to remain a dumb animal for three millennia. *For no good reason!*

The best of men cope with our stunted situation. Many fall into despair. Many resort to violence in words and thought, if not in actions. In actions, often enough. None succeed fully at being human. None walk away unscathed.

It makes sense. How does one feel a sense of love when the most incredible experience of love cannot be shared with another? How does one react? How does one remain human?

The woman never encounters the failure to give (which makes it so difficult for her to understand). Experiencing that most amazing feeling and not being able to share it is far more damaging than sharing it while not achieving it. How does a man avoid selfish results when a loving act is turned into a selfish act? How does one avoid bitterness once it is realized that the end game is missing? This last applies to both genders. Over a lifetime, we cannot avoid the awareness, even though it is shunted to the subconscious. Our awareness will not be denied.

For early humans, how could they cope with such a complicated thought? Humans were just doing what animals had done for eons. Their essential difference had not yet clarified.

Humanity came up with the most nonsensical conclusions regarding coitus, sex in general, and all of human life. It has spawned endless horrors. All because early men could not learn what it takes to last long enough to love a woman.

Love was stopped cold in its tracks. Humanity could not cope with the situation, so it threw the whole subject under the bus. We made excuses, bizarre explanations, and distractions. As our awareness grew, so did our desperation in absence of resolution (which was due to hiding from the problem!).

Even so, we have sensed all along that there is something more to our existence. That has caused the schism to widen even further between our human nature and the prehuman condition.

Maybe an even better way to say it is our *preexisting* human condition. The condition we inherited from animals without changing it in the most significant way.

The issue was initially so forcefully suppressed that we never gave it any real thought. As it was shunted aside, so was our humanity.

A lot of heterosexuals hate the idea of non-heterosexual sex. Why should they care? Why should they react in such an offensive manner?

The purpose and intent of most every other form of sex *is* mutual orgasm, the sharing of a loving experience.

It highlights the problem from which humanity has been desperately trying to hide. We'd rather squash anything that makes the problem more apparent than attempt to address the problem. Idiotic, at best.

The great subconscious fear has always been that the great stupid secret our really stupid ancient ancestors created would be revealed. Idiotic, at best and, ultimately, destructive.

Unassisted heterosexual intercourse (i.e. coitus) is not mutually orgasmic in 75% to 95% of the cases, no matter what the fictional books and movies suggest. The evidence, in the form of studies, has been building for nearly a century. Coitus is not working to a sentient race's threshold of acceptance.

Can you see the conflict that the subconscious awareness of this causes? The rationalizations that whittle away at our humanity and stability? The subconscious admission, whether we like it or not, is, "I'm terrible at coitus, the foundation and most pure essence of joy in sentient life. I cannot share the orgasmic experience with anyone." The thought cannot be entirely avoided (though most will try for a lifetime). It erodes a sentient being's existence and consciousness.

It is no wonder that sentience and sex were blindly cursed by our ancient ancestors (as is often still the case) in the absence of resolution.   Unfortunately, it became cast in stone and tied around our necks for millennia. *It is the basis of human misery.*

Just think about it.   What could be more devastating to a sentient psyche?   A man simultaneously achieves the most incredible experience in existence while leaving the woman undone.   Both are disappointed repeatedly and regularly throughout a lifetime.   It may take a little while to sink in but, oh, inevitably, it does.

The otherwise incredible experience of climax shunts any thoughts regarding the accompanying failure to the back of the man's brain.   Just go to sleep and don't think about it in the morning.   For women, it has been an increasingly frustrating situation since it began to dawn on our consciousness.

That's okay.   I've done the important thinking for you and every generation to come.   You're welcome.   Don't squeeze the glands.

Give it a generation or two and there will be no questions left. It will become second nature within a couple of generations.

Coitus can *only* work well for a sentient being. Animals were stuck with a dumbed-down version that suited them.   Humans were given conscious awareness to perceive the true situation and the intellect to change it into something truly wonderful. We can adjust.

We cannot avoid the conclusion that coitus should be loving, so we have no other choice. We must adjust or remain stuck in a bizarre existence somewhere beyond the animal but well short of our humanity.

There is another side-effect as we stumbled and became blinded to the truth. We began to think of love as only some vague, ephemeral feeling. Love is based on sharing and giving. An advanced form of caring that no animal can ever imagine. How can we love and learn to care at an accelerated sentient level when we cannot *share* the most incredible loving experience of human existence?

An animal's primary function is to have sex, make babies. A sentient being's *additional* function, that distinguishes it from other animals, is to *make love*, engage in coitus that is mutually orgasmic and fulfilling for both, as well as make babies *as and when* it makes sense.

This creates and maintains the foundation for a copacetic, stable, emotionally balanced state, beyond the dog eat dog world that we know so intimately.

Rather than women finding every way in which to avoid coitus and men finding every which way to avoid the truth, all we need to do is learn to make love.

The mistake we have always made is believing that all we need is love. No. All we need is to *make* love.

So much of our activity remains driven by an animal's brute, mindless, vicious mentality. The awareness that we should damn well be a loving race, while enduring our horrible lesser state, only compounds the problem, sending us further into despair and dismay.

To say it has been driving us mad for more than three thousand years is an understatement. To say it grinds away at our situation ... well, look around.

It all stops right there. All of our magnificent success is for naught until we become human. We must perceive what is really going on. We need to gain our balance and stability.

The man shrugs his shoulders and says that's just the way it is and the woman shrugs her shoulders and says that's just the way men are. Neither sees the source of love, much less its lack. Neither understands why some women have it in such abundance and most men have a hard time scraping any together.

All of the pursuits of life will continue to be sought. It's just that it won't remain mad pursuits to substitute for a fulfilling life in the absence of love. An environment that begins and ends in love fits our human nature. It stabilizes everything.

Kudos to the many, many couples that remained relatively stable without the reinforcing physical aspects of love. It was well done. It was just never enough. It has been plowing through life rather than experiencing the full panoply of a sentience existence.

Women give and men take. It all starts in bed. It need not be that way. It *must* not remain that way.

I could have taken the approach of just publicizing how to achieve loving coitus but that would never have overcome the undermining nature of the deceits that encourage a man to avoid the subject altogether.

Loving coitus

Humanity becomes human when it learns how to make love, in the literal as well as the sexual sense. Another misfire was never realizing the defining nature of the term *'make love'*.

This also shows the profound depth of our conscious awareness that we produced such a term even though the loving act remained absent. *Mutually orgasmic coitus makes love!* It's just incredible that we coined the term and ignored its obvious intent.

Loving coitus is an evolutionary imperative to rid us of the blind ambition of the animal and replace it with a sentient ambition amidst a loving foundation.

It is not genetic. It is a matter of conscious awareness leading to resolution through the use of intellect. It is a new type of evolution that Nature provided. Is that awesome or what?

A unique, thoughtful, emotionally stable and distinctly human awareness is to accept that both genders *can* attain orgasm. Mutual orgasm, in whatever way it is brought about, is making love. It begins to make us human.

Loving coitus is making love in the most natural manner possible. It fulfills human nature like no other. Eye to eye, the man and the woman are fulfilled. They become something more.

It is human to desire mutual orgasm and love. We seek it for a lifetime. Making coitus into a loving act has proved virtually impossible until now, *because we were to afraid to look*. We turn out the lights, instead, or seek alternatives.

Every generation goes through the same disorientation. As they approach puberty, they have the highest expectations. As they reach puberty, it all falls apart.

Bewilderment and despair begin to take hold. Each generation rebels in their youth, not even knowing what exactly they are rebelling against.

In our youth, we sense that something is missing. We know not what. The ongoing failure finally wears away any resistance to the inevitable misery.

Each generation, then, finally caves and becomes the next generation to accept the nonsense and misery of a sentient creature that remains an animal out of its depth.

Worse yet, as we age, many decide to take it out on the world. Just look around. It is happening in a big way as I write. Witless hate becomes a common outlet.

Repeated failure and a growing sense of despair forced our distant ancestors to suppress the subject of sex. No one wanted to face the failure.

Coitus, the primary form of sex, is the *only* form of sex that seldom ends in mutual orgasm. It is an inevitably miserable situation. It is instrumental in creating the disruptive, derogatory characteristics of our prehuman condition.

That Nature made sure that loving coitus *is* possible for a sentient race is beyond remarkable. Nature did not leave us hanging. We did.

We will become human when we no longer desire to turn the lights out and, finally, open our eyes during coitus and fuse into something more as a loving couple. Into something human.

There is no longer anything from which to hide. It is just instincts, blindness, and the obfuscation of our ancestors that prevented us from realizing how easy loving coitus is.

A sentient race has no other choice but to overcome its animal instincts regarding coitus or continue down a destructive path. Once sentience made it clear that there can be more to coitus, there was no choice left. Humanity has misled itself into destruction and frustration ever since *for no good reason!*

The mind has been educated but not the heart.

Surprisingly, few of us ever experience loving coitus consistently, if at all. We are not talking about a fair state of arousal but full on, set-the-spine-on-fire orgasm for *both*. Anything less is a disappointment to both sentient beings and excused as the best that can be done. How horribly wrong we have been.

The official estimates of failure hover around 75%. My own estimate hovers much closer to 100%, for a number of reasons that are scattered through the series of books.

We do not even take seriously the possibility of loving coitus. This is reflected in the research that studies premature ejaculation. Two minutes is defined as success at overcoming premature ejaculation! Women need more like seven to fifteen minutes. Add to that the fact that there are no suggestions other than hold on for all you're worth and you begin to get the picture.

Do not think that the best a man can do is hold on for all he's worth. That is an animal's answer to a human problem. The whole issue was misdefined as overcoming premature ejaculation.

What is really desired is *indefinitely delayed ejaculation.* That is a completely different question that produces a *completely* different answer.

Animals are born to misery with no relief. We are not. We immerse ourselves in misery because we have not accepted what our sentient awareness has been telling us all along. There is more to coitus and a sentient race.

For an animal, it is only about relieving an urge and allowing its instincts to tell it what to do. To achieve our humanity, it takes something more. It takes accepting what our sentient awareness is telling us and, then, doing something about it by applying that sentient awareness and intellect.

The biggest problem is overcoming the many millennia of deceits put in the way of considering the issue clearly. Understanding how to perform loving coitus is not difficult at all, once placed in context.

Coitus should be able to hold its own in *love-making*, not just making children. We are too smart not to realize that coitus can be full-on loving for a sentient race.

Without it, we remain a demented and very dangerous animal. We cannot survive well under such conditions. We may not survive at all.

So, why in the world is enjoying loving coitus not the standard? Why does it remain necessary to make a choice between mutual orgasm or coitus?

Loving coitus is the natural progression provided by nature that has been impeded by our (animal) instincts and never admitting to our fears (of failure). This prehuman state is bounded by our forced blindness.

In the absence of loving coitus *or* any other form of mutual orgasm as the accepted standard in relationships, all manner of monsters appear to fill the vacuum that remains.

For those sudden spasms of fear that it can't be done, I assure you, it can. First, though, I had to convince you that I'm not selling anything but our humanity.

Every time I try to describe how a man can last indefinitely, I feel like I am trying to sell something. I am certain others feel the same. *I am not*.

I'm not even going to copyright this book. It's too important to limit its availability in any way.

If it weren't for all of the brainwashing that we have endured for millennia regarding the act of coitus, my twelve years worth of books and mind-wracking effort would not have been necessary. The answers would have been obvious long ago.

It is not improving the act of coitus that is difficult. It is overcoming all of the nonsense that we have developed over three thousand years.

I have always chosen loving coitus. Since it didn't exist, it nearly destroyed me. *Nowhere* could I find any hint that a man can last indefinitely. <u>Any man can</u>. *Everything* we *believe* convinces us that coitus will remain a failure. It need not. It is pure nonsense.

Essentially, we are so averse to discussing details about coitus that, of course, it took forever to break through.

Why were we so averse? Well, that is another long story. In short, call it confusion of the highest order between what the *animal* knew to be true because of a track record of a billion years and what the sentient creature sensed but could not articulate or elucidate, much less resolve, that created feelings of bafflement and embarrassment. We were initially too uninformed to do anything but hide.

We couldn't avoid coitus, so we made up stories (that is, lies) and reinforced those stories over the millennia. We became so desperate that we reinforced the situation by creating blind obedience to supernatural laws of behavior and omission of thought. We created vast empty vistas of thought that were to be avoided on pain of reprisal. Sex was cursed. So were you if you spent any time thinking about it.

The unspoken rumor grew that nothing could improve coitus. So, why talk about it? Instead, we scattered the remnants of our sentience and went full tilt into superstitions and deceit.

Coitus should be celebrated. Instead, it is something we don't even want to think about.

Many kids frolic through life up until they hit puberty. Then, it all goes to hell in a hand-basket. We mislabel it as maturity. It is accepted that adulthood equals misery.

In *Millennium*, I discuss armoured innocence. It is not the innocence of a child. It is the fully aware innocence of an adult that has been inoculated: by the fulfillment of loving coitus, clarity of conscious awareness, and reliance on one's own integrity that remains in tact; against all of the nonsense that we have tolerated for millennia.

Sex has been treated as a shame, which is just insane. The most celebratory act of being human and we treat it like a disease. Worse yet, the whole script has been flipped!

We have finally gotten to the point that we can discuss sex rather openly but that took about three thousand years. While we talk about it, we *still* steer clear of the real issue: coitus.

Because we steer clear of the main issue, any discussions on sex are a jumble of nonsense that arrive at insane conclusions.

Coitus, in its current state, doesn't stand up to the close scrutiny of a sentient race.

I am sad to say that you still probably don't get the point: coitus should be everything we imagine (in our youth). That changes the world!

Coitus can provide mutual orgasm without any assistance, acrobatics, pills or appliances and it makes all the difference in the world.

It is wrenching, once you realize that all that have gone before hadn't a clue what it means to be sentient.

If you are older, you should revel in the knowledge that humanity is close to attaining its humanity and you may be blessed enough to attain love in full measure. If you are in your youth, I envy you. Your life has a very good chance of being completely human and seeing love flourish.

We are sentient. That means we notice things that the other animals don't. Like the fact that the female of the species *can* achieve orgasm, which the prehuman never wants to admit due to its erroneous certainty of egregious failure. Instead, we bundled misinformation into superstitions and became mad (in every sense of the word).

As the situation became clear, it caused a hurdle to be placed in the way of sentient reasoning. Prehumans had a new challenge ... and they failed utterly to face it, much less achieve it. This is not a knock on those early men. It is just circumstances due to the transition from animal to human. Our whole past was so painfully inevitable.

Nature really knows what it is doing. It gave man everything needed to easily overcome the failure.

Let's look at it from yet another direction. Long ago humanity couldn't quite make heads or tails out of the sexual situation. Guess what he passed on to his ancestors? Not much except fear of admitting failure and the subliminal desire to avoid the subject. This is what every generation has rebelled against in its youth and reinforced as it aged.

Youth has always had high expectations (rightly so) for loving and sex. Then, it all turns to ashes as they reach puberty.

To speak for all men: "how in the world can it be that I cannot make a woman moan in joy during coitus??!?!"

It damn near killed me, more than once. Worse yet, a man doesn't know if his fellow man can or can't. He's not about to ask. He just knows *he* can't, which makes the situation all that much worse. Multiply that by almost every man on the planet and you may begin to get the picture.

The lack of mutual orgasm further erodes a relationship as it continues. The sex becomes perfunctory The failure dissolves all of the aspects that would, otherwise, fuse the two into something more than a disgruntled relationship of tolerance.

In 'grown-up' lingo, the prehumans have matured enough to realize that life is miserable. Just get used to it. Right. And, then, you die and are thankful for it. Great plan.

Once we become loving, we become different. We become what Nature intended all along. We will have educated the heart as well as the mind.

I am beginning to become utterly convinced that it is the gazing into the eyes of one's lover that awoke our sentient awareness. The ability to look into the eye's of one's lover during coitus is all but unheard of among animals.

Go back all the way to the beginning, all the way back to the days when we first transitioned from animal to prehuman. We began to become aware of so much more about our existence. The transition really gained momentum as we began to express ourselves in words.

We come full circle. First nature awakens us to the uncomfortable feeling that something is missing by making it natural for humans to engage in the act of sex while gazing into each others eyes.

The next step is to figure out what is wrong and create its human equivalent, loving coitus, *for which nature provided.*

Humanity is far more than a trumped up animal. We just haven't put all the pieces together yet. Sentience is about the heart (emotions) as well as intellect (which has also been debilitated to a great extent). Our emotional instability is all due to the lie we have been living for three millennia.

Ever since we emerged as a species different from the rest of the animals around us, we have struggled to distinguish ourselves as more than an animal in anything other than our intelligence and our ability to wreak greater havoc.

We were trying to contend with an animal's situation but humanity had brought something new to the situation (our conscious awareness) without accounting for it.

If you are at all like me, you wonder about the human condition occasionally. In my case, I spent a lifetime studying it. We have been missing the big picture. While you may have been puzzled by this or that, I was puzzled by the whole setup.

Only over the last dozen years did it become clear what is really wrong. In my previous books, you will note that I lash out at a lot of the nonsense. It was my way of purging humanity's demons. My fury, when I began to realize I had been duped for most of a lifetime, purged the demons well.

We have followed one awful misconception to its bitter end since we first began to use our brains for other than surviving. We followed a foregone (and wrong) conclusion because the animals before us accepted a situation that is unacceptable to our conscious mind.

Then, humans cast the misconception of the animal into words and began to create nonsense to be taken on *faith.* It had always been that way (before humans), so why should anyone expect it to change?

We accepted a notion that turned our sentience upside down.

I am expecting that you are prepared, at this point, to learn how loving coitus is achieved without being repulsed. What should repulse you is the awful *pre*human condition that we continue to accept in its stead.

<u>*Details*</u>

The Leap Never Taken

If any man had ever taken the time to think instead of scurrying into the darkest corner to hide from his shame, he would have realized it is not *his* shame.

It might have been an animal's shame, but they are too witless to care, even if they are aware of the failure. Who knows?

For a human male, though, he has enough sense to think, if he is only willing. He is not witless, but he is very, very aware of his failure.

He has been discombobulated by the inertia from the past. The hopelessness was passed on him from his witless ancestors.

Everyone is convinced that the man is on some kind of a countdown clock. Sure, the clock starts ticking for an animal or a human male *that doesn't think things through*.

First of all, every man worth his salt has the evidence right in front of him that the clock can go into suspended animation. Any man worth his salt has, errrr, taken care of things for himself, on occasion (rather than having it happen at an embarrassing, inopportune moment).

Did you ever notice how difficult it is to even get the clock started in such a case? There's a reason for that and it hints at why that clock should be completely under the man's control.

Of course, you will say, "but that's not the same!" *Exactly*.

There are actually a few differences between rehearsals and engaging with a woman.

One difference is that one cannot tickle themselves. That is, essentially, what happens during 'rehearsals'. That is what makes skin on skin such a glorious event, unmatched by anything else in life. The erogenous zones, essentially, has elements similar to the two well-defined ticklish responses in other areas of the body. In this case, the muscles triggered are those in the crotch. That is critical.

There are also other differences, as well. They all add up to a man being able to make love the way he has always dreamed *if he takes the time and effort to think things through.*

Another difference is that when engaging a woman, there is movement that is usually missing when one 'rehearses'. That movement, when studied, makes it clear what is happening, why the animal has *no* control *and* why the human can.

An animal operates by instincts. Let me interpret "instincts" for you. Instincts is the inability to think. It is doing something the same way it has always been done *because you are not thinking it through.*

Sound familiar? It should. It is the overall way in which we have operated for millennia. Like a witless animal.

One mistake *the animal makes* should be glaringly obvious but, somehow, it seldom really hits home. There is a driving urge for a man to dive as deep as he can. It is often even encouraged by the woman. It is a really good feeling.

Unfortunately, it triggers the *approach of climax.* Save it for the grand finale. It will be the finale, whether it is grand or not.

If you remain an animal, it is called rutting. It is done without thinking. It is done way too early for a human.

The musculoskeletal structure is set up to begin the discharge process when you dive deep.

In essence, it is all about the glands in the crotch that contain the vast majority of the fluids that make up the discharge of semen. When those glands are squeezed, Bang! You're done.

Even without the deep dive, there is one more instinct that must be avoided. This one is a little more subtle.

The muscles in the crotch, surrounding the glands, when flexed and released, squeeze the glands in a couple of ways. They do not need to flex and release. This will take a little more effort than "don't do that". You will actually have to think it through.

There are two ways this 'pumping action' can happen. Both are nothing more than instincts of the animals that came before us that can be overcome easily - *if you can think like a human.*

Animals perform those actions because they *can't* think. We perform them because we have not thought.

Men don't think it through because they never realized it was nothing more than instincts. No one told them any different. Well, I'm telling you, DON'T.

The two actions? First of all, the muscles in the crotch are flexed during the movements of coitus *without thinking.* The muscles in the crotch *are not necessary for movement.* They are only flexed during movement because we never think about it. With just a little forethought and practice, a man can easily avoid using them during coitus. The muscles in the legs, back, torso, etc provide all movement *without* the use of the pelvic muscles.

It takes practice, of course, but the crotch muscles are independent of movement. You don't flex them because they are needed for movement. You flex them because no one ever really thought about it because we were all acting like scared little children unwilling to look under the bed.

Secondly, the 'ticklish' (erogenous, if you prefer) response. The muscles in the crotch get very little exercise. While performing the particular movements of coitus, it is dangerously easy for those muscles to inadvertently and unnecessarily spasm in response to the mind-bending erotic 'tickle sense'. The skin on skin action is similar to tickling a person's feet with a feather or the more intense tickling of the muscles under the arms. It is a challenge to avoid flexing those muscles due to this, but not impossible. The same holds true of the muscles in the crotch.

It is far from impossible. It's just something that no one has ever spent any time studying. So much for 'mystery'.

It takes a *little* forethought and a *little* regular exercise of those muscles in one's crotch to be able to prevent the unwilling muscle contractions. That's it. The exercise makes the muscles more supple. The forethought and practice make them responsive to your commands (including unresponsive to the ticklish reaction except as desired). That's all there is to controlling those muscles and, thus, controlling ejaculation.

I came up with the terms, "don't twerk" (i.e. don't dive deep) until the lady sings (i.e. is ready for her own climax or climaxes) and "don't jerk" (i.e. don't flex those muscles in the crotch) to make the concepts easy to remember.

If you are not enraged by the fact that this has been there all along and, somehow, your ancestors never got a clue, don't feel alone. I was burned for a lifetime. I hope you catch on sooner. My fury, once I discovered the dodge game we have played, nearly consumed me.

As one learns what they are doing, unless the woman is doing her best to catch you off guard (which may become a great game to see who can outlast whom), it becomes easy to last as long as one desires. Can you imagine coitus as a loving, fun event?

There is, of course, a lot of fine print. It is no big deal. Only one more regarding early discharge. It's also the easiest to understand. If the glands are overfull, nothing it going to stop them from being squeezed and, thus, beginning discharge. No different than the bladder being in the same condition.

The other fine print is the woman's anatomy. If you want to be her lover, if you want to make love to her, for the first time in your life; the first time in the long and painful history of humanity; if you want her to climax, you will also want to learn a little about her anatomy. I cover that, to some extent, in some of the other books.

One of the big surprises for the unaware is that the most erotic zone of a woman is *outside* of her love chamber. It is just above, usually less than a couple of centimeters or half-inch. If you aren't paying attention, you may very well miss stimulating it at all. The rest? Within an inch or so, just inside the opening.

Why, then, is the deep dive so enticing for both the man and the woman? Ummm, it is an incredible feeling? *As is mutual orgasm* (not necessarily simultaneous, though that might make a nice goal). Save it for the grand finale. It's the icing on the cake for the humans that finally can make love.

The other aspect that I will stress, I am certain will need no emphasis one we become human. A man is easily aroused. A woman, at least in our prehuman condition, not so much. Your efforts to arouse her need to be in everything you do. The way you touch her, the way you look at her. The way you communicate with her. In essence, the way you romance her. Romance is far more than the effort taken to get her in bed the first time. It is the effort that should last a lifetime of love. Oh, goodness, you will be able to spend a lifetime gazing into her eyes as she transcends this existence right along with you. I am so jealous! ... In a good way. ;~j

Part II

Loving coitus is just a matter of our sentient awareness understanding what causes the discharge of ejaculate to begin and, then, recognizing and overcoming two instincts and one animal response that cause it to begin.

The point is to avoid ever *starting* ejaculation rather than holding on for dear life *after* ejaculation has already begun. Once it begins, it is all but over.

Men have *always* accepted that *starting* the process of ejaculation was impossible to avoid, much less control. **_Big mistake_**. We have looked away from the issue of controlling ejaculation for millennia because the thought scared men spit-less due to past failure to control. The hopelessness was passed along from generation to generation. It is time to get over it.

Men have carried these reactions around without realizing their impact on their humanity or, at least, avoided the realization due to the unsubstantiated feelings of hopelessness. Dumb animals carried them around for millions of years before that.

The big picture is that the sex glands in the crotch, when squeezed, begin the process of ejaculation. Also in the big picture is the fact that we are sentient. We can overcome anything that we put our minds to. This one situation *that finally makes us human* and differentiates us from the animal decisively and conclusively has never been considered seriously, until now.

Two instincts and one animal response that cause the sex glands to be squeezed have never been accounted for.

Men have just held on for dear life rather than study the anatomy and those characteristics of the act of coitus that produce the unfortunate results of uncontrolled ejaculation that ends the act of coitus before it becomes a loving, thereby, human event that creates the loving environment that is human.

By studying the anatomy, it becomes clear. Squeezing the glands in the pubic area begins the process of ejaculate discharge. Period. That's it! Two instinct and the spasming response of the pelvic muscles make it happen.

The erotic spasming response of the pelvic muscles, similar to the ticklish response of other muscles, potentially, *not necessarily*, contract to squeeze the sex glands in the crotch.

This response is probably the most elusive characteristic of the orgasmic response. When uncontrolled, it can cause a twitching of the orgasmic muscles in the crotch, which squeeze the sex glands. When consciously aware, a *human* can control that response. The spasming of the muscles involved is not necessary until orgasm is achieved through ejaculate discharge.

The response of the muscles in the crotch to the sexually erotic sensation *can be controlled* by *anyone* that is consciously aware (it is no more than a part of the movement that I term 'jerking').

It is only due to humanity remaining unaware of the response that made it seem impossible to overcome. It was unaccounted for. It can be consciously controlled by any human. If you cannot control the response, you are not yet human. Most men have yet to achieve their manhood and humanity. The exercises described below can help you become familiar with the sensations that lead to the end and overcome them.

There are also two instinctual reactions that cause the squeezing of the sex glands in the crotch. These are even easier to overcome, once identified. The unfortunate end result is the same, the early end to what would otherwise be a loving act.

It's that simple. The real issue has always been the forced blindness. Our consciousness remained subjugated to the millions of years of the animal doing it wrong because we were too afraid to look closely.

One of those instincts is as simple to implement as it is to understand. Men don't twerk until the lady sings. Women should. Thrusting the pubic bone (crotch) forward squeezes the glands decisively. The man's *instinct* is to immediately plunge as deeply as possible. Women often never move at all or only slightly for fear of causing the experience to end too soon and being blamed for the early end. The woman should twerk for all the man can bear.

In the case of twerking (undisciplined full forward thrust), the musculoskeletal structure forces the pubic bone into a position that squeezes the sex glands, as well as causing the pelvic muscles to contract. It will invariably cause the end of coitus.

The second instinct is much more subtle. The pelvic muscles have *nothing to do with movement*. The pelvic muscles do not *need* to flex. When flexed, they squeeze the sex glands.

If not under conscious control, the muscles in the crotch (pelvic muscles) *will* flex. It's not so much leaving them lax as *not flexing them.* Flexing and un-flexing those muscles acts like a pump. Spasming due to the 'tickling' effect causes the same results. It is all about control of one's own muscles for the man.

These muscles have nothing to do with movement nor do they need to react to the stimulus of arousal or penetration. There is no reason to flex them, other than instinct and unfamiliarity with those muscles.

The muscle response or deep plunge squeeze the glands containing the fluids that begins the cascade to orgasm. Save the deep plunge for the finale, when *she* is ready. It will *always* cause ejaculation and orgasm on call and in seconds.

Holding on for dear life is *exactly* what a man does not want to do as it amounts to *flexing the pelvic muscles!*

I'll reiterate: *don't squeeze the glands!*

One more critical point. If the glands are <u>already overfull</u>, squeezing the glands is unavoidable. The solution is obvious.

With responses in play, it begins and ends in seconds. The responses are rarely, if ever, *consciously* considered. It's time to learn to consider them and overcome the animal.

The man must keep his thrusts relatively shallow until the *intentional* finale. Only about two inches is required to stroke the woman's every erotic nerve-ending inside and out. The shaft strokes the most sensitive arousal point (i.e. clitoral nub) that is just outside and above the opening as well as the clitoral wishbone, much less than two inches inside. Stroking the wishbone, just inside the vaginal opening, with the flaring portion of the head will also help stimulate the woman. That may be best saved for after have learning the basics. The woman's twerking assists her orgasm in the same way as a man.

Just be careful and go very slow until you understand 1) how deep is safe (it should be far more than two inches as you progress) and 2) how to avoid contracting (and, especially, spasming) the muscles in the crotch.

An additional technique, if necessary, is to stop all activity at the first sign that you are becoming overstimulated until the sense of overstimulation is gone. It should not be necessary with exercise and avoiding twerking and jerking but may be useful while still learning. You may want to refer to 'edging'.

It is a learning process. We are human. That is what we do. That is what we are *supposed* to do. In the case of coitus, we have avoided the learning process, thus remaining a dumbfounded animal.

Anything beyond a neutral position is too much (at least, initially, while you are learning to adjust to being human). It takes far less than neutral position to stimulate the woman's crucial erotic zones while *not* squeezing the glands, thus avoiding the beginning of the end.

With experience, a man learns what depth won't squeeze the glands while learning how to avoid muscle contraction and spasm.

These points are straightforward and become natural. It will become as natural as the instincts and animal responses that they replace within a generation or two of the time that humanity begins to succeed at love in its most essential form.

Arousal itself and penetration can also triggers pelvic muscle spasms (flexing, by any other name), if one is not familiar with the muscles. In other words, all that is required is being master of one's own body. This is why I recommend exercising those muscles to achieve familiarity and mastery of the muscles.

The exercises are just as crucial for loving coitus in youth as it is for later in life. There are other benefits as you age, like not wearing diapers. The immediate advantages, even in youth, include making it easier to control spasming. It will take some slight effort and discipline to avoid flexing and spasming. Avoiding the deep plunge is just a matter of paying attention.

In case you missed it, you are human. Controlling those responses are as easy as walking on two legs. Now, you will be able to open your eyes to the one you adore while loving her.

I like to spend *two* minutes (only two!) exercising those muscles daily, and, also, *not* flexing them, while moving the muscles that *are* meant for movement. On the back with knees flexed and swinging towards each other and away works well.

Flex and un-flex the pelvic muscles for thirty seconds in pulses. This will help you become familiar with the ticklish response. Then, hold them flexed for another thirty. Then, leave them relaxed for another minute will working the leg and hip muscles.

Another good, errr, non-exercise is standing knee bends *without* flexing the pelvic muscles.

In essence, you are trying to do two things. Condition the pelvic muscles *and* become familiar with *not* using them when unnecessary and detrimental to the loving act of coitus.

You might also want to look up 'Kegel exercises'.

There will be more to learn about avoiding flexing as you make love but this will prepare you by becoming familiar with the act of leaving those muscles relaxed while flexing the muscles necessary for movement. I'm sure a more complicated exercise could be conceived.

Another caution. Self-stimulation needs to be done carefully for the man. If you abuse your member, it will come back to haunt you. *Do not inadvertently do so!*

There is no reason to do so, *if you realize what triggers an orgasm.* It can be difficult to achieve orgasm when, errr, taking the matter in hand *because* the normal motions of coitus are *not* the norm during self-stimulation. Also, the tickle response is absent if, err, taking things in hand.

Also, the urge to rush through it can become a habit that follows through when attempting to last as long as *she* desires.

If one uses something other than one's hand, it will be possible to engage the tickle response and begin to overcome it. Abuse will make the spasm response *extremely* difficult to overcome.

Humanity should learn to approach masturbation unabashedly. It is far better than letting the lack of release get under one's skin. I'm not expecting that to change in a hurry.

The most important things to know are: don't twerk or jerk (i.e. dive deep or flex/spasm the pelvic muscles, respectively) until the lady sings; control the spasm (tickle) response; become familiar with the pelvic muscles and control them. Just remember, you are human. Of course you can control them. Keep in mind that overfull glands means they are already squeezed. Do not become discouraged if it takes a little while to adjust. The older you are, the more time should be expected in order to adjust, there are more bad habits necessary to overcome.

You can now proceed to engage in mutual orgasm enthusiastically in a human manner while gazing into your lover's eyes. Love can finally mature into its sentient form.

I apologize for concentrating on the men's issue but they have the most to learn, by far.

The *only* difference is the woman might want to work on accelerating her orgasm - or not. Just make sure you are doing the opposite of what I've recommended for men and you should orgasm. Flex and twerk like crazy. As much as he can bear. Relish the erotic feelings that cause the spasms to engage.

I am becoming more and more convinced that, as we open up and become more comfortable with the change and the insights, we will learn a lot more.

As one example of the physical aspects, though, it may very well seem obvious that the 'neutral' position I mention is not nearly as important as not flexing those pelvic muscles. But, the deep plunge is certain to cause ejaculation and orgasm.

All of this will become natural. We will no longer be in hiding, and we can look for further ways in which to improve the love. I don't mean just the physical aspects, either.

As an example of the other aspects to explore further, I'll mention romance. That is another natural aspect of being human that has been inhibited by men's inability to love physically. Once our natural desire to love is established and reinforces, the rest of our loving nature, in every form, will come to the fore.

The Trouble With Troubles

There is something disturbing humanity at a fundamental level. That disturbance keeps all of the nonsense in motion.

If you inspect closely, what we have tried to do regarding is focus on each little individual trouble that humanity causes and stamp it out. We have tried to contain the chaos in only two ways: laws and religion. They only attempt to *contain* the havoc.

Both start with the assumption that we are irretrievably screwed up. Then, *both* attempt to put a lid on the pressure cooker of the *pre*human and never consider becoming human.

The pressure cooker still explodes regularly. It is boiling as we speak. May we survive the next explosion to become human, since I don't think we can turn on a dime.

Both religion and laws are *outside* forces. *Internal* turmoil is not addressed. We either punish or brainwash. Neither works well at all.

Loving coitus, or any form of mutual orgasm, addresses the *internal* turmoil. *That* is a force to be reckoned with. External force attempts to make us *act* like humans. Loving, *making* love, *makes* us human.

Loving coitus restores the natural self-respect and self-image. *That* unleashes our conscious awareness and humanity.

Our hearts need to be educated, our emotions stabilized, our conscious awareness liberated. *Then*, we have addressed the acts of the animal.

Our humanity is not something we just casually dismissed. It is something we rejected with prejudice due to the initial stupour of the animal as we first emerged into sentience.

The situation also created the inequitable situation between the genders. There is no reason for it to continue. Men have had an inferiority complex and they took it out on women.

It should be obvious that the tension starts with the couple. It ripples out from there to distort everything.

Nature had a higher level of bonding in mind for the human all along. It just requires a sentient race to accept that which its heightened awareness makes painfully clear.

In most cases, there is the question of which came first. In this instance, not so. Coitus came along long, long, long before humanity's heightened awareness and rumours of love - by a factor of about a *million*.

Our heightened awareness made us uncomfortable with coitus and its results. We, as sentient humans, cannot avoid the conclusion that there is more to coitus. Our inability to face what our awareness made appallingly apparent undermined our humanity. We pass on all of the awful nonsense from generation to generation, like a witless animal.

Evolution

We have always thought that our only evolution had to do with our intellect. We have been missing the evolution of conscious awareness. Our emotional state remains a shambles because of the inhibitions our conscious awareness, which also leads to inhibitions of our intellect. They are intertwined.

All of the research on premature ejaculation confirms what I have been saying. Our conscious awareness and intellect were hijacked to avoid confronting a serious failure.

We don't know what we are talking about _and we don't want to!_ The only possible point of lasting longer for a man is to please a woman, so why proclaim lasting two or three minutes as success? Women need more like seven to fifteen.

How could we have avoided realizing _for three thousand years_ that a man can extend ejaculation _indefinitely_ if men's awareness _and_ intellect were in tact??!?!? Instead, we celebrate that _some few men_ can last two minutes! Ridiculous!

We are currently thoroughly convinced it is not possible to last long enough to please a woman! We are up to our eyeballs in nonsense. The **_unintentional_** sidebar conclusion is that the _woman is not worth it._

Our sentient awareness has never been comfortable with any of this. It was handed down in such a fashion that it derailed men's sanity from birth and wrecked humanity. Can you smell the desperation, fear, misogyny, violence, and disappointment?

Darwin and the theory of evolution never took conscious awareness into account. Conscious awareness is a new form of evolution. It supersedes genetics.

To let coitus remain an animal's act is to deny the evolution created by our conscious awareness and intellect that can finally makes us far more than an animal. We are not a dumb animal. We are just acting the part.

A sentient creature has no real option. By the _nature_ of conscious awareness, we are aware that coitus can be much more. It is thrown in the face of our conscious awareness repeatedly throughout a lifetime.

We are far too dangerous to stay as unstable as our prehuman condition portrays (especially, as anyone in their right minds can see in the 2020s and a few years preceding, no matter which side of the ludicrous fence you sit on).

This failure to make coitus into something human is at the core of all of our instability.

Instability is *not* part of our human nature. We are far better than that. The instability is pure animal with a side dish of madness *because we are no longer just an animal but have yet to attain our natural loving, human state of nature.*

In other words, it is beyond the dim-witted animal's ken. Animals don't go mad because they haven't the wit to realize what is missing. *We do.* It *drives* us mad.

To paraphrase from *Millennium*, the evolutionary change between neanderthal (or ape, for that matter) and modern man is nothing compared to the conscious evolutionary changes over the next one hundred years as we learn to love.

Nature

Look at the big picture with all of this in mind.

Nature has directed life towards intelligence and love.

I call it the trajectory of life. It begins to make one wonder if Nature has an overarching intent. As if Nature has an agenda.

Nature set humanity up in such a way that it could overcome *all of* the limitations forced upon the animal.

Nature made a race that could gaze into the eyes of its mate during coitus to make certain that it became and remained aware that something was missing. Nature also provided the equipment to ensure that coitus *could* become a loving engagement. It is truly remarkable.

It has always been up to us to perceive reality and fulfill the sentient state by making coitus into a loving experience.

Nature seems like an incredible symphony at times. Does it have more in store for future generations, once we become human? It seems almost certain.

Significance

For the longest time, no one seemed to catch on (I'm talking millennia here). It was an embarrassment that no one wanted to mention. As the realization and comprehension has grown, men have become more dispirited and unstable; and women have become more disgruntled and frustrated by their treatment, station, and disregard.

Less than a century ago, no one would even acknowledge that the issue of coitus' failure for a sentient race existed. As our awareness continues to grow, the certainty that something is wrong with coitus grows more and more painfully obvious, as does our precarious state (though many will still deny both).

The misdirects are legend. We don't even think about it as coitus being broken. The topic we will discuss endlessly, now, is that *sex* is broken, never even referring to coitus (pick a side on *that* ridiculous, myopic argument). Of course, since the main topic is absent from discussion, all kinds of nonsense is bandied about. If coitus is mentioned, it is uttered quietly or indirectly like poking a bear.

The instincts of the animal during coitus mixed in with our raw, undeveloped sentient awareness that initially contended with the situation has taken humanity for a ride for many millennia. We have gone to great lengths to avoid the real issue but it is always there haunting us. It's time to get to loving.

Lifetimes

If you consider the perspective of lifetimes, maybe it is easier to understand. Let's start with the individual human's lifetime.

A human lives, maybe, one hundred years. When a human first comes into the world, they don't know a thing. They are, then, filled with notions that they find out later in life are a sham. They feel betrayed. The expected bliss of an intimate coital relationship blows up in their faces as they reach puberty. The disgruntlement grows over a lifetime. Only the exceptionally perceptive see behind the curtain before it is raised (not me).

Then, let's look at the lifetime of humanity. We grew up as a species amidst an animal mentality. The sexual instincts are trained right into a man's spine from our earliest predecessors.

Making the leap to realize it is only instincts - not genetic edicts carved in stone - that move those muscles during coitus, is, in essence, simplicity itself. The realization was blocked at a level that doesn't allow any consideration of the situation.

That it take us so long to figure out is such a sure sign that it was a huge disturbance over the millennia. The fact that we hid so desperately from the situation just shows how destabilizing the thought of failure is. It has defined our past.

We have been holding back the tide of our sentient and loving nature taking full control of the human condition in order to finally reflect our human nature.

There is a myth that suggests we only use 10% of our brain. Not true. 90% of our brain is spent dealing with all of the nonsense we have concocted over three millennia to rationalize our failure to become human.

We could be putting all of our brain power to use for something exceptional, like true *human* progress that does not destroy everything around us. We are bent on destruction and now you know why. We hate remaining only an animal for good reason.

Being human and loving is not some mantra or conscious effort. It is a natural state of being that is empowered by self-respect, self-confidence, and self-love. It is denied by self-loathing.

The human, loving state flourishes with sentient clarity. The noble characteristics of humanity, like honour and integrity, are crushed under the boot of self-loathing.

Do you get how big a deal this is? The long term effect?

What we do has to make sense to us. It doesn't yet. As long as it doesn't, we cannot become human. We remain prehuman.

It is not enough to intellectually understand what is needed (e.g. love). A mantra of love is good in the face of monsters does nothing. It only rescinds the individual's acceptance of what is really going on. It is self-interest, self-salvage and, ultimately, self-destructive. Proclaiming love is good is like ... well, you make the analogy of inconsequentiality.

Our humanity is not defined by intelligence alone. It is also defined by unobstructed awareness and stable emotions. Anything less is prehuman, a demented smart animal only. Just look around or read widely the comments on twitter.

It has been a fight every step of the way. We hem and haw because we get weak in the knees every time we try to consider the most important subject. Or, we get uncontrollably angry.

We have been trained since birth to avoid realization. As we turn twenty and, then, thirty there is a fundamental destabilizing factor as puberty and hormones gain a full grip and emphasize what is missing, while the conditioning makes it impossible to even consider. The real situation remains buried in our subconscious. Make no mistake, it still remains.

We are sentient. Our sentient nature, our human nature knows better. It is begging to be set free.

We get so caught up in the minutiae that we never see the big picture. We play whackamole with each little transgression as if that were all there was to it. It is a species-girding demented phenomenon. Sure, some overcome the worst of the denigrating force. That doesn't make them more human. The misery remains. They know they are failing. They just accept it in misery and reduce their lives to the minimum to save some small shred of love. Others rage and wreak havoc on all and sundry. Both are miserable. One admits it. The other just blindly rages.

We have yet to move beyond the animal in any significant way. Don't look around at all of the toys of humanity. They are not what makes us human. They are doodles that any animal with an enough brains could create. Like weapons in every imaginable form and enough paranoia (also due to...you guessed it!) to make sure we use them.

About three thousand years ago we started getting a clue, a hint that there is something more. We called it love and failed to make any significant progress in achieving it over all this time.

Performing coitus in the way that it was intended for a sentient being will make the race loving and human. Not witless love but precious, priceless, fulfilled love.

Men's Nightmare

It's a man's world, they say. It is also man's nightmare that he shares with everyone. It unhinges a man's mind as he remains caught between the instincts of an animal and his human potential. He has carried that nightmare around with him for more than three thousand years.

Men

Did you ever wonder what the hell is wrong with men? They create such awful messes. Men have boggled, bamboozled, confounded, and conned *themselves* since the beginning. Everybody pays for it.

They convinced themselves they are no better than animals and never looked back.

Once the nightmare has ended, it won't be utopia but it will be a hell of a lot better than this cockamamie version of existence.

Men need to realize that the whole thing is a ruse (that they caused themselves, no less!). Men feel emasculated. That is the nightmare. They feel that way because they are. Because each generation is programmed with an animal's fear never to delve further, they remained that way for more than three millennia.

Three thousand years ago, someone had the wit to figure all of this out. They wrote Pandora's box. Someone knew *three thousand years ago (!)* that there was more to the story. But, the lid was closed.

The hope still remains. I have opened the lid to let you peer inside. It is up to you to bring it out into the world.

A Tale

Trying to explain what happened with sex is attempting to tell a story of millennia. You have to take it apart from the present and work your way all the way back to when we transitioned from animals.

So many insights have been accelerating over the last one hundred years. As it all began to become clear, as we finally put our foot down and said, "enough!", it has begun to drive us mad because we could not see the light at the end of the tunnel. We have broken into more and more shards of insanity.

It's hard to say when we figured out where babies come from. It seems even animals might have some sense of that. They may also have some sense that coitus is incomplete. Watching bucks chase after does and the does wanting nothing to do with it (same with just about any other species of animal) and the bucks banging into anything in their way makes one wonder.

What is certain is that coitus, orgasms, babies all existed long before humanity did. It had a track record. What humans didn't seem to accept was what their heightened senses started detecting regarding the anomalies about the sexual aspect of being alive. That misstep has cost us our sentience for millennia.

As far as dating the realization, Pandora's Box and *Kama Sutra* date it to around three thousand years ago.

I remain amazed by the myth of Pandora's Box. It is such an accurate description of our ongoing dilemma. Pandora's Box is our conscious awareness. When we 'opened' it, chaos emerged in the form of the realization that coitus was incomplete. Hope for resolution was left in the box. We closed the lid on it and our sentience. We hid from it in confusion and embarrassment.

Over the millennia, we hammered nail after nail into the lid of our conscious awareness. Every time it would try to peep out, we would hammer another nail into it.

The Garden Of Eden is another matter entirely. That myth modification squashed any thinking on the matter, any form of resolution, and *blamed women for it all!* It is so sick, I shake with fury every time I ponder the pompous male attitude of failure and excuse! (If there were any doubt, I am male.) The only reason that must have occurred is fear. It certainly nailed many significant, heavy duty nails into the coffin.

We are supposed to perceive the universe better than any species before us on Earth. While we do okay with comprehending the universe, we have obscured the view of our own humanity to such an extent it it has taken me six books and seventy years to unearth the truth regarding our precarious position.

We have never peered closely at humanity itself. Not seeing through to the tight link between coitus and love completely blurred our image of humanity and its potential. It distorted our sentient perceptions on the highest order affecting everything, even how we perceive our place in the universe.

We have crystal clarity regarding sex and coitus as an animal would view it. The transition from an animal's viewpoint to that of sentience has (I hope) just begun.

Humanity *needs* to learn to apply the phrase agapé to itself.

Reorienting the focus to all that coitus can be was far beyond our ancient sentient ancestors comprehension. That caused a serious snarl (in both senses) to our ability to see clearly.

Be certain you realize that this change spans *the love of a species for itself* (because the individual cannot love itself) right down through to the individual and intimate, fulfilling relationships that can exist within a loving environment.

It's stunning as it all falls in place. With the phrase "intimate relationships" I don't mean just intimate sexual relations. I mean that every relationship can start from a place of love.

I know. It sounds mushy - today. At best, it is an intuitive description in which humanity will fill in the details. I just don't think I will take the time to figure out how to say it less mushily.

We have been hobbled by the encumbrances of our animalistic past and our unfocused image of human nature. We only perceive our animal legacy with crystal clarity.

Not because it is cooked into our genes but because we have not committed to our conscious awareness that we can be so much more. We cling to misery with tungsten claws.

We have moved beyond genetics. It is now also about conscious awareness and realization. Honest, clear conscious awareness surpasses genetics by a long shot.

By avoiding clarity, all of the misery is endorsed. From the awful treatment of folks that try to find some way to love another human in a physical manner that includes mutual orgasm to misogyny, the overall mistreatment of women, and the irritable disposition of men. All of it seeps through our humanity making for the awful prehuman condition. It all stems from our inability to face the fact that the animal rendition of coitus is found wanting by a sentient, self-aware race.

Just the open admission that coitus does not provide mutual orgasm in its current form begins to put us on a stable footing. At least, we are acknowledging the truth.

All of the evidence is there in books, in studies, research, and on the web. You just have to look and put the pieces together.

Our *real* dream comes true when we realize that a man *can* last as long as *she* desires. It seems such a small thing and, yet, the consequences are tremendous.

Our concentration should have always been on indefinitely delayed ejaculation rather than overcoming the specious premature ejaculation, the few seconds that is the norm for an animal, by two or three minutes. Until we attend to indefinitely delayed ejaculation, we remain animals. Demented ones at that.

It is not some difficult course that takes years of experience, practice, and learning. Young men should pick it up in a hurry. Older men may have difficulty overcoming their habits. I can attest that it can be done.

All of the 'research' and 'studies' performed so far have been nothing more than desperate action to avoid, not answer, the questions that no one wants to face. We forced the issue into the subconscious to avoid confronting the reality that our sentience made crystal clear. It's insane.

We are a race that became acerbic because it has never found its sentient footing. Loving coitus provides that stable footing and so much more. Without it, sex remains a curse and we remain a demented animal.

If anyone gets what I am saying here, we will have found our footing. They might walk around in a daze for a little while as they take it all in, of course. I did. We can, then, quickly pick ourselves up and shake ourselves free. The reason I say if anyone gets it is because if anyone can get it then anyone can get it. I hope that's clear enough. ;~j

Equivalency

Every form of sex was conscripted by animals long, long ago. Except one. Loving coitus. It is only for humanity to make loving coitus. That we haven't achieved it shows just how little we trust ourselves and our humanity. Both genders desperately want mutual orgasm but we don't trust ourselves to figure out how to provide it in the most elegant manner possible.

It may surprise some women to realize men don't like the situation any better than women. How could they?

Men are driven to sexual release by more than just instincts. There are physiological processes, like the buildup of semen, that make it imperative for the man to seek sexual relief. That he cannot fulfill the act in the way that he desires, of course, drives him to distraction and mad (in both senses of the word).

There is no doubt, by the way, that substituting pills for manhood is a debacle. It does not provide self-respect.

Little or no explanation will be required as it becomes second nature. It is just that we are so tied up in knots by the nonsense consumed since birth and the despair endured since puberty.

Young men of the future will pick up what to do and the confidence to do it just as they pick up the fear and awkwardness on the subject today. Through osmosis. Fathers will no longer fear that conversation with their son. They will finally be able to provide answers, if necessary, rather than awkwardly stuttering.

Arguments

Oi veh. Sex is a mess. Humanity is a mess. The former caused the latter. It is so simple to say and, yet, so difficult to comprehend or, even worse, attempt to convey through the obstructions in the mind that are immense and intense.

I had to reach such an intensity over the last dozen years that I have a difficult time describing the state it put me in.

I had to break down so many nonsensical arguments, then fit the answers into the picture. Like I've said, we don't want to talk about. We don't want to think about it. We all have our stock responses that keep us from having to think about it at all and put anyone off from asking further questions, leaving the important conversation dangling for three thousand years.

Many that have daringly taken alternative routes to assure mutual orgasm have an almost militant attitude due to all the flack they have had to endure. Understandable, but not helpful.

I smashed against all of those rocks many times.

I finally found a jigsaw puzzle analogy to describe the effort I have been going through for the last dozen years.

It has been like looking at a jigsaw puzzle in which everyone just mashed the pieces down irregardless of whether they fit or not. So, I come long, look at the puzzle, and finally realize it is an incomprehensible mess.

That was about a dozen years ago. Since then, with the overall answer in mind, I have attempted to inspect each piece of the puzzle and rearrange the puzzle into a coherent whole, while anyone I encountered adamantly attempted to jam their piece of the puzzle back in place where where it was, while avoiding the big picture. In other words, I received no help, only self-justification.

Put enough of the nonsense arguments together and one can begin to get a clear picture of the mess we call home. I can't say

I've sampled culturally across the world to the depths that I would like. It's not terribly important, though.

One thing is clear. This involves all of humanity and the little differences around the world in various cultures just don't matter. It affects all strata of all societies.

Our disruption is all due to the nonsense of accepting the legacy of animals. It is a gift that keeps on giving as long as we tolerate its insanity. I go much further into the details of all of this in the other books. This is more like a snapshot.

The only way that we become human is if indefinitely delayed ejaculation becomes the commonly accepted practice of performing coitus. Get over yourself and read that sentence accurately. If you have some other way you prefer, go for it. That's not the point.

I have always been certain that loving coitus was crucial. Awareness is good, resolution is critical. If I had not found how to alleviate the failure, I would not have published the first book.

That is why I worked so hard to find a way to make it simple to do so. I have done just that.

The scope of all of this is obviously huge. One has to start (which I noted in the very first book!) with the assumption that the misery and foul prehuman condition does *not* reflect human nature or its needs. We have been living a nightmare.

Of course, there is a spectrum of reactions by men but all of them sum up to the same thing. A constant irritant and disruption to a man's self-perception that scales to half of humanity, for all intents and purposes. Whether he succumbs to misery or rage matters little regarding the big picture. His self-love (or, self-respect, if you prefer) is slowly whittled away. It limits his humanity in one way or another and creates disgruntlement and disruption for all. We remain less than human.

One of the strangest and, for me, *saddest* results of this awful state is that too many women have been convinced that it is all their fault (shades of Garden of Eden).

One of the most *awful* results is that many women are beginning to mimic the male toxicity, since resolution seemed (past tense) to remain unattainable.

Retaining one's self-respect by learning to love enables all of the admirable qualities of our sentient state, like honour and integrity (a more robust list of these characteristics are in previous books) that we have discussed endlessly for ages with little apparent success. We never understood the source of our humanity, love, and noble characteristics. It is the physical form of love that is missing and critical.

For me, I wanted to bring a woman to orgasm while gazing in her eyes more than anything in the world. I am not alone in that desire. Now that desire can be fulfilled.

I emphasize that it is not men's fault but, still, the results are in. The most immediate curse and apparent disaster due to the lack of loving coitus is the destabilization of men and the offensive way in which women have been treated.

Lousy coitus insinuates itself into every crevice of our existence. Resolving it will not make everything bliss but it will rid us of the main irritant that causes humanity to go on rampages. *It will greatly reduce the disturbances that we cause for ourselves because men are in an irrational state.* It is humanity, *not nature*, that causes most of the havoc we endure.

More so, there's that wasted 90% of our brains. I know that may seem excessive but it seems true as my mind clears all of the nonsense.

While my attempts at clarity are meager, the long term effect should prove out. Forget the percentages, we will finally be able to think. We will think clearly regarding humanity, our horrific circumstances, and our goals, for the first time in our existence.

Let me approach misogyny from a different standpoint. Sometimes, I'm convinced no one realizes that misogyny is a gender wide phenomenon. This truly blows my mind.

Misogyny is stitched into every fiber of the fabric of our prehuman society. It is stitched so deep it clearly has an ancient and widespread origin. It is also clear that it was not the initial setup. Women were honoured, adored, and celebrated in our distant past before something turned it all upside down. I peg that at less than three thousand years ago.

Even though many men make quiescent noises, it takes the will of the majority of the gender to stitch it so deeply into the fabric society.

The laws, regulations, and preaching to ameliorate the effects do not change the actual circumstances. The underlying distortion and motivation remains. The laws are an outside force. They only dampen the madness and not very well at that. Laws are the codification of the training that women have always attempted to provide men. This only puts a cap on the rage that always, always burst forth from the prehuman male.

Look around in the 2020's. The rage, once loosed, extends itself well beyond the boundaries of misogyny. It ranges far into the realms of insanity. Make no mistake where the rage begins.

There are so many pursuits that reveal that we haven't learned a damn thing. We still pursue life everlasting rather than life that counts, as an example. Some are still just waiting until they are dead for relief.

We are built on circumstances. The biggest circumstance of all is that maybe as high as 99% of humanity gets cold-cocked at the spry young age of pubescence with nowhere to turn, never to recover. That is when our brains get thoroughly highjacked for life. I don't think *anyone* is stupid. We have all been stupoured. At times, it really pisses me off.

It's not so much that men are trying to prove themselves to be men (though that is the common understanding - even among men), it is that they are trying to distract from their failure as men by creating a facade of 'manliness'. All of the past rituals of attaining manhood are just that. We are virtually all compensating in some form for the lack of loving coitus.

There is only one way to resolve the issue. There is only one way to completely countermand and eliminate the distortions to our human experience. It's important. It is a serious distortion to the thought processes. It short-circuits everything.

Most importantly, though, loving coitus completes us. I can't prove it, though I have done everything I can to explain it. Only time can prove the case. I am certain that it will hold up, at least to gain us the next level of existence in this universe.

Humanity *wants* to love. Right now, the effort is led by women and cut off at the knees by men. Not the paltry, on again-off again, thing we call love today. But the robust version of love that can permeate our existence that only a fully, clearly sentient being can experience. It *requires* sharing love on a physical level. That is where love gains its full measure.

The bovine correlation between life and misery stems from the fact that life, in the absence of loving coitus, is inhuman.

The way people react to any attempt to discuss coitus tells the story clearly and I've had lots of those conversations. Don't get me wrong. I was just as prone to the brain-washing. Only my growing rage and unwillingness to accept all of the offenses to our humanity allowed me to burn through it all.

Most people I talk to, including a person that reviewed a few of my books, seem most intent on defending their own choice rather than considering the impact of loving coitus on humanity.

Brains shut down because of the failure. It took me more than forty years after puberty to begin to face the truthful, awful state of our prehumanity and why it is so.

All I have ever encountered is someone (including heterosexuals) with a stock answer that requires no thought (an overall hallmark of our pre-sentient state) or, in the following case assures no thought, "God did not make women to enjoy sex". Many carry on this witless argument.

No. Nature made coitus so animals could not, for the obvious reasons that they are dumber than oatmeal and their only goal must be to make babies.

Nature provided humanity with everything required to make coitus into a loving act of mutual orgasm. Any man that says differently is cowering from his own failure.

From the anatomical capability to the awareness and intelligence to realize the situation, improve it, and adapt, while still providing for procreation, Nature, in the form of sentience, changed the game. It allows us to be so much more than an animal. It allows us to be human. Any other view is cowardly.

The other logic that tickled me was, "Yeah, you really need to find a man that is willing to go down on you".

No one sees the bigger picture! At least, women have a good excuse. They can't do much to engender the necessary change, though I feel they have gently been hinting at the problem since the beginning (e.g. the term 'make love').

But, still, anyone that has adopted cunnilingus should be in the first wave to learn how to love thoroughly. Why perform such an awkward act when one can love a woman eye to eye?

There is *nothing anyone* can say against making coitus the loving act that we have always claimed it was and, to our awful disappointment, found it was not, while never even admitting the latter.

Only loving coitus has the clout to change our conditions into something that empowers our human nature. It seems clear that was Nature's intent all along.

That does not mean other forms of sex will not continue. It just means that, without loving coitus as a backstop, we fail.

The animal

Let's take a look at some of the residue of the animal that we unnecessarily hold onto. "Everyone for themselves" is a huge one. "Kill or be killed". "Might is right". "*'Falling'* in love". Do I need to explain why these are animal utterances?

I'll explain one, since it is a big one on which much of our nonsense has been erected. "Only the strong survive" is a real favorite of the prehuman animal. Of course, it's not true, even before humanity existed. A more accurate statement would be that those most suited to existence survive.

That awful belief has been used to justify the worst nonsense of the prehuman condition. It is used to bring us to the brink over and over again. You can shout against it all day (just as you can shout "love is good"), make laws all you want, and it still comes home to feast on prehumanity regularly. There is only one way through. Become human.

A sentient perspective that is accepted without fail makes humanity more suited to survival. Conversely, remaining an overly intelligent animal without the liberation of conscious awareness and insight leads to destruction and not much else.

Our humanity is an evolutionary transformation, which we have yet to achieve. As long as we take it on the chin like an animal, we have not evolved and we add risk to our survival. As long as we avoid what our conscious awareness makes unavoidably clear we are not accepting our circumstances. We are not well suited for survival. We remain an unbalanced race.

Our conscious awareness is a given. Without accepting *everything* that it tells us, we are a failure.

Everything wrong with humanity begins with men not learning that they can easily last indefinitely and provide loving coitus. *That* changes the game.

Until we accept the game that Nature handed to us, our existence will remain a misbegotten distortion of an animal's existence full of confusion, frustration, anger, stupour, a virtually nonfunctional brain, and a willingness to lash out at the slightest provocation.

We have outgrown the animal and if we do not realize that, we destructively fail.

Connecting the dots

The big dot that initially led me in the right direction was realizing that only about two in ten men (as documented by others; maybe a little more, maybe a lot less; maybe one in a thousand would be my own estimate) can last long enough during unassisted coitus to allow the woman time enough to achieve orgasm (remember, the goal of most studies is to last two minutes, not please a woman). Once I realized that, all of the other dots I had collected over a lifetime crystallized. So many incongruities and quirky qualities of our condition began to make sense. This is covered in some detail in my earlier work.

Misery

The misery begins with men's vague awareness that they are failing to love a woman thoroughly. That unease and the way in which men attempt to compensate has been growing for millennia. Sooner or later, the lid is blown off, once again. The easy answer is, "we're just an animal, after all." The right answer is to find human resolution, which I have provided.

End game

Many idealize romance as something to be sought out - even if it can only be found in movies. Happily ever after and all that.

Like so much of our whackadoodle prehuman existence, we have flipped it upside down. We have misconstrued the intent of romance.

Romance, in the form of seduction, is not human. It is a form of prehuman subjugation and dominance, much like the buck and the doe.

Romance, once we become human, will be a form of caring that is created to deepen the love of a couple *over a lifetime*. Not just used to get a woman in bed. It is a natural extension of love.

Love is an advanced form of caring only available to humans. It is initiated and fulfilled by loving coitus. It expands to fulfill humanity.

La difference

I have stated repeatedly that *some* of the finer traits of women are just human traits, rather than feminine traits (only some!) that have been mostly absent in men.

We conclude that it is a feminine trait because of its absence in men. It is so often absent in men because they revert to the animal, more often than not.

That in no way suggests that there are no differences between the genders. It's just that we have confused the traits that are human and gender based.

Let me give one example. The discipline that men will require to achieve loving coitus will give them very specific trait of, let's say, willpower and discipline. So much better than toxicity.

Or, the incomparable feminine trait of bearing children. That is a feminine trait, for sure, and gives them qualities that no man can ever replicate.

Vive la difference! I can't wait to see the actual traits and differences between the genders of an unobstructed sentient human race. It will be awesome to behold.

Finale

Love becomes an interesting study when the noble characteristics (like dignity, honour, integrity, compassion, empathy, etc.), that have also remained mostly in arrears, are considered in context. They are all well-defined yet remain unattainable as standards of behaviour. Love, we can't even put clearly into words.

This is because we have been running away from the source of love while running, madly and blindly, towards its limited, broken animal equivalent of lusting and rutting.

Everything insane about the prehuman condition has one root cause.

I have tried, again, to show how important this is. In this instance, I tried to show it from a high level.

I have tried to ease into the subject in a way that can counter all of the nonsense you have been fed (and fabricated yourself) for a lifetime. I hope I succeeded. It is the most difficult effort of a difficult lifetime.

This book is more like a brief, whereas the other books are my in-depth exploration of what went wrong and my attempt to straighten out all of the crossed signals of the prehuman condition.

I was still pondering the puzzle and where each piece fit.

I was purging the nonsense from my own brain while, simultaneously, attempting to explain to the level that I understood at the time.

This book clearly describes our situation as well as seems possible. It describes why our situation remains a disaster and how we get out of the rut in which we have remained for millennia.

Equipped with the clarity provided by this book, the others should not be too much of a challenge. In other words, if you got this far, you should be good to go.

Just remember, in the previous books, I was exploring with the intent of achieving the clarity that I hope is conveyed in this book. Yes, with each book, I really thought I was being clear enough (rolls eyes).

I wish I could provide the earliest version of *Sentience*. It was full of "may be" and "seems to be". It would show you just how tentative I was at the time I initially delved into all of this.

I did not go into this lightly. I did not just throw down whatever popped in my head to justify my own existence. It was my third or fourth attempt to make sense out of the mess we call the human condition. The previous attempts led nowhere. They were outside forces.

In the initial version of *Sentience*, I was slapping down all of the tentative ideas as quickly as possible because they were all flooding in at the same time. Then, I had to go thrash through those ideas over and over, again. I rewrote *Sentience* at least twenty, maybe forty, times. It wasn't editing. It was rewriting.

There is no question left in my mind as to the source of all of our upheaval, our nonsensical existence, and the gap remaining before we achieve our human, loving nature. I hope I have conveyed it clearly enough for you to accept.

The most important (and clearest) information regarding how easy it is for a man to last indefinitely is in this book. I go through a lot of details, further insights, and discoveries regarding that subject, particularly in *Millennium* and *Sentience*.

I'm sure there is more to learn. There is enough here, though, in this book alone, for any man to be a lover in the most natural manner possible.

As with anything of interest that hasn't been mystified into its grave, there is always more to learn. Loving is high art or will be, once men can take pride in their ability to love.

Endings

It has been an incredible dozen years. When it first dawned on me what was going on, it was like this huge *click* in my mind.

It seemed crazy initially, but it kept falling into place. This fits *everything*. If you comprehend what I am conveying, as you begin to look around at life, it will become more certain for you. It fits all of the quirks that you see daily that make us less than human.

Every book, every movie, every human interaction makes sense under these conjectures.

The previous books are explorations of the topic. This is the big picture. Today, our existence is based on our animal legacy.

We never look at the very obvious big picture that humanity itself is very, very broken.

In less than one hundred years, our humanity could be based on love. I hope so, anyways. Please excuse any mistypes or awkward transitions. There was no editor.

w

Thank you for reading this book

whickwithy@gmail.com